D0726648

– AFTER DINNER GAMES –

Lagoon Books, London

Series Editor: Simon Melhuish
Editor: Heather Dickson
Written & researched by: Jenny Lynch
Page design and layout: Linley Clode
Cover design & illustration: Gary Sherwood

Published by:

LAGOON BOOKS
PO BOX 311, KT2 5QW, UK

ISBN: 1 89971 242 9

Printed in Singapore.

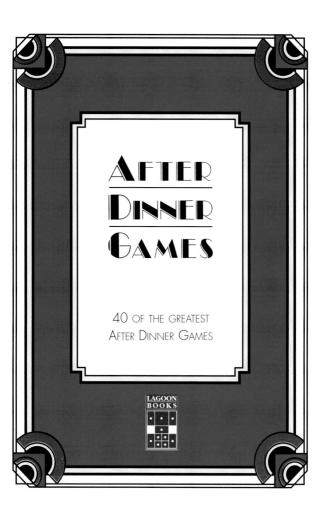

AFTER DINNER GAMES

40 OF THE GREATEST
AFTER DINNER GAMES

LAGOON
BOOKS

— **I**NTRODUCTION —

Whatever the occasion, whether it's a family knees-up or a friendly shindig, there's an after dinner game to suit everyone in this fun-packed book.

There's nothing quite like a party game to break the ice and even amongst people you've known for years, a team game can introduce a bit of sparkle and liven things up.

Tried and tested by a team of party-animals, these 40 After Dinner Games are guaranteed to bring hours of entertainment and plenty of side-splitting laughter.

All you need to take part are the people, the place and a few household objects to act as props.

The 40 different games in this book have been divided into four sections.

Pick a few games from each section and your party is guaranteed to be a success!

Section 1 ~ Table Games

These are reflective games which can be played as you sit around the table. Some require pencil and paper, others just a ready wit. They are perhaps the more "learned" of the games, but not exclusively so.

Section 2 ~ Lively Games

These are slightly more lively games than those in Section 1. You can still play these whilst seated round the table but you may need to push the debris into the middle to make way for frantic gesticulations. Some games call for quick thinking, others a great deal of bluffing.

Section 3 ~ Riotous Games

These games require the players to leave the table. Most are team games and entail a lot of shouting and general hullabaloo.

Section 4 ~ Late Night Games

These games are best attempted late at night. They contain physical stunts and races that you would never dream of attempting in the cold light of day but which seem to be particularly amusing late at night. As long as players have some sort of control over their limbs they should enjoy these.

INDEX

TABLE GAMES

A popular Victorian game requiring players to waffle on about a given subject for exactly one minute.

BBC Radio's "Just a minute" programme and various board games have updated and popularised this game enormously.

Everyone thinks of a topic for a one minute speech. It could be anything from The Evolution of the Gardening Spade to Modern Manners. Each player writes a subject on a piece of paper, folds the paper and puts it in a hat or bowl. You will need a host who acts as timekeeper and who can settle disputes.

The host reads out one of the titles and the first player then has to speak for as long as he can (maximum one minute) on that subject. Other players listen and can make challenges for:

HESITATION ~ if the speaker stumbles incoherently or cannot find the right word

DEVIATION ~ if the speaker waffles on aimlessly about an unrelated subject

or *REPETITION* ~ the speaker can only repeat words which are in the title (Obviously, words like AND or BUT can be said as often as needed)

If a player challenges correctly he can then take over the speech. Whoever is speaking at the end of one minute earns two points, whoever has the most points at the end wins the game.

BE WARNED: deviation can be an extremely contentious challenge. The speaker is allowed to try and justify his waffle but all disputes are to be settled by the host. The challenges are what makes the game most fun and should be encouraged. You will find that the role of 'speaker' will change repeatedly and rapidly!

To play, all you need are paper, pens, a hat or a bowl and a watch with a second hand.

— OTTICELLI —

*One of the greatest games of all time,
this is brilliantly suited to dinner parties.*

One player thinks of a famous person, dead or alive, fictional or real and tells the rest of the guests the first letter of the surname (for example – R for Buck Rogers). The other players take turns to ask indirect questions to try and discover the identity. They do this by thinking of someone that it could be and then asking a question about that person – but NOT a direct question.

So if Player 1 thinks it could be Ronald Reagan he might ask *"IS IT AN EX-PRESIDENT OF THE USA?"* to which the answer would probably be *"NO, IT IS NOT RONALD REAGAN"*.

As long as the player is able to think of any ex-president whose surname begins with R then that is the end of Player 1's go.

If the player has a mental block and cannot think of any suitable ex-presidents then he has to admit this and Player 1 then has the right to ask a direct question.

Examples might be *"IS THE PERSON DEAD?"*, *"IS THE PERSON MALE?"* or *"IS IT A POLITICIAN?"*.

Gradually a picture of who the person might be is built up.

Once you think you know who it might be, you can not ask directly *"IS IT BUCK ROGERS?"* unless you have won the right to ask a direct question by, for example, asking first *"IS IT A FICTIONAL HERO OF THE 25TH CENTURY?"*. Whoever guesses correctly can choose the next mystery person.

It is not a good idea to pick Elvis Presley or Madonna as these will be guessed quite quickly but *'THE POPE'* or *'KING KONG'* should keep people guessing.

— Forbidden Letter —

A word game which does not require any physical exertion and can be played while everyone is still seated round the table.

Players decide on a letter of the alphabet which is to be forbidden. From that moment on, players are not allowed to say any word which contains the forbidden letter. Each player is subjected to a question and answer session lasting three minutes. You can either appoint one person as the questioner or, to make it more fun, all take turns to ask a question. Of course, the questioner also needs to abide by the rules and avoid the forbidden letter.

Every player starts with five lives and anyone who has any left by the end of the game is a genius.

Obviously, the choice of letter will determine how hard the game is. It is probably best not to start with a vowel but it does need to be a letter which occurs relatively often.

— GUGGENHEIM —

An excellent 'categories' game.

Players decide on between six and a dozen categories, for example: colours, flavours, foods, countries etc. These are written in a list down the left hand side of a piece of paper.

Then a "KEY" four-letter word , for example "BOWL", is chosen and written across the top of the paper.

Players now have a grid which they fill in by finding a word for each category which begins with the letter in the key word which heads each column. Thus in the first column in our example, a player might write down: brown, bitter, bread, Bulgaria.

After 15 minutes players stop writing and take it in turns to read out their answers. Score two points for every word which no-one else thought of and one point if one or more of the other players also have the word.

Once you've got to grips with Guggenheim, you can experiment with more difficult categories. TRY: parts of the body, dances, battles, biblical characters, words containing the letter K....

To play, all you need are paper and pens.

— EVER ENDING WORDS —

*A testing game in which players take turns to call
out letters which form a word – BUT the object is NOT to be
the person to finish the word.*

The first person calls out a letter. The player seated next to him calls out a second letter which might go with it to make a word. The third player then adds his letter. Play continues with each player contributing a letter, still having a genuine word in mind, but avoiding finishing ANY word.

Each time a player calls a letter out he should try to have a word in mind. Thus the next player inheriting S, A, T might call out 'I' (thinking of 'SATIN' and trying to trap the next player). (Three letter words do not count so the person who adds T to S. A. doesn't need to go out).

If a player has inherited a difficult group of letters and cannot think of a letter to add without finishing a word he can either accept defeat, or bluff by adding a random letter with no word in mind. Players are allowed to challenge a dubious addition, but it is only the next person to play who can challenge at any one time. A correct challenge wins the game. An incorrect challenge knocks the challenger out of the round and play resumes with a new word.

The object here is to bluff like crazy. Announce your letter with verve and confidence and you might just get away with it. You may need a dictionary on hand to settle any disputes.

To play, all you need is a dictionary.

 — Never Ever —

A very simple game that is nonetheless very amusing to play.

Player 1 starts by saying *"I HAVE NEVER..."* and goes on to mention something which he has never done. It could be:

> *I HAVE NEVER USED A SUNBED.*
> *I HAVE NEVER READ A NOVEL.*
> *I HAVE NEVER EATEN AN ARTICHOKE.*
> *I HAVE NEVER IRONED A SHIRT.*

The aim is to think of something which you haven't done but which everyone else will have done. So, depending on your friends, things like 'ROBBING A BANK' or 'SEEING THE LOCH NESS MONSTER' are probably not a good idea. The object of the game is to be as inexperienced as possible. If you manage to think of something which everybody else has done then you score one point. If someone claims that they also haven't done whatever it is, then you do not score any points.

This is best played amongst people who know each other fairly well as it's the only way to be sure that people aren't tempted to lie! Dishonesty is absolutely forbidden. Points can be deducted for lying.

— Poet's Corner —

A game that is played a little like "Consequences".

Each player has a strip of paper and writes two lines of poetry at the top. This could be something they have made up or the opening lines of a Keats sonnet! Players then fold the paper so that only the second line is visible and pass it on to the player on their left.

The game continues, each person receiving one line of poetry and adding another. It does not have to rhyme but if it does, so much the better. A set length should be decided on – say, eight lines. When this is reached, the papers are unfolded and the poems read out.

An alternative version is to compose limericks. Each player should contribute one line and these can either be written down and passed round or players can try improvising 'on the spot'.

There was a young lady from Stroud
Whose parents were terribly proud
Always a winner
She came round for dinner
Was obnoxious, offensive and loud.

THERE WAS A MAGICIAN FROM BATH
WHO HAD TERRIBLE PROBLEMS WITH STAFF
THE FIRST ONE HE CHOSE
WAS A WOMAN CALLED ROSE
WHO SQUEALED WHEN HE CUT HER IN HALF.

This can become addictive and is the sort of game that people keep coming back to. If you can include the names of other party guests, so much the better.

To play, all you need are paper and pens.

— SAUCY CROSSWORDS —

*This game makes no claims to be highbrow
but it's guaranteed to provide a laugh.*

Players take turns to throw the dice. Highest score goes first. The first player has to write down a word with the same number of letters as the score on his dice. It should be a 'rude' word. The next player throws the dice and has to think of a word which will fit in with the first word, again the number of letters in the word is to be dictated by the throw of the dice. Play continues round the table.

```
B   O   T   T   O   M
U
R
P   A   N   T
```

Modesty prevents me from presenting a really good example but I'm sure you get the drift. The best thing is the heated arguments that ensue as to whether or not a certain word is considered 'rude' enough. Challenges should be encouraged but you may need to appoint an adjudicator to settle disputes.

To play, all you need are paper, pens and a dice.

— TELEGRAMS —

A game requiring quick thinking, often with hilarious results!

Players call out letters in turn which everyone writes down. Up to fifteen are needed.

Players then have to make up a sentence using each of the letters called out, in the order in which they were noted.

L S B U G U T P Y M

might yield:

LOVELY SEXY BARRY URGED GRANDMA UP THE TELEGRAPH POLE YODELLING MADLY.

or

"LET'S SING BEAUTIFULLY, URGENTLY AND GENEROUSLY", URGED TREVOR, THE PIOUS YOUNG MAN.

Use of conjunctions and the word "the" can also be used where necessary.

Players should be encouraged to include the names of those present: be as imaginative and wicked as you dare.

After a one minute time limit, everyone reads out their version. Much disagreement will probably ensue as to which is the funniest.

To play, all you need are paper, pens and a watch with a second hand.

— WORD BLUFF —

Also known as 'Call My Bluff', this game requires some advance preparation, but it is one of the all-time great after dinner games and well worth the effort!

You will need a list of obscure words – the more unusual the better. Each one should be written on a piece of paper with the correct definition. Some examples are given on page 19 but you can add as many as you wish with the help of a good dictionary.

Players form two teams and the words are dealt out between them. Each team should then spend some time making up two alternative false definitions for each word and writing these down. When everyone has had enough time, teams take turns to read out their word (be prepared to give the spelling if necessary) plus the three definitions. The other team members confer and decide which version they think is correct. One point is awarded for each correct guess.

The real fun lies in making up the false definitions which can be as far-fetched as you wish. You can make them sound terribly learned or just plain ridiculous but all should be delivered with a stony face which reveals nothing!

For example...

What do you think D A S P Y G A L is:

i) a German beer

ii) an adjective describing hairy buttocks

iii) a medical term referring to the way one's toes wrinkle after submersion in water

To play, all you need are paper, pens and a dictionary.

Some Examples For Word Bluff

PEDICULOUS
(adj) infested with lice

WILLIWAW
(n) sailor's name for a sudden violent storm

FUCIVOROUS
(adj) subsists by eating seaweed

GLABELLA
(n) the smooth area between the eyebrows

FORMICATE
(v) to crawl like an ant

DOTTLE
(n) plug of tobacco left unburnt in a pipe

SUDOROUS
(adj) sweaty

VALGUS
(n) person with a deformed foot

LIVELY GAMES

— Cheat —

*A classic card game guaranteed to bring
out the worst in people!*

Deal two packs of cards out amongst the players. The object of the game is to get rid of all your cards by whatever means is necessary. Cheating is, of course, positively encouraged.

The first player lays down as many cards of the same value (for example, threes or fours or fives etc.) as he wants to in the middle of the table and calls out what they are, *"THREE FOURS"* for example. The next player has to follow by either laying more cards of the same value, or any number of cards of the next value, in this case fives. The point is that the cards are laid face down and any player can lie about what he has got rid of.

A player can be challenged by any other player. If challenged, the player must reveal his cards. If a lie is discovered then the cheat has to pick up all the cards that have been played so far. On the other hand, if the challenge is incorrect then the challenger has to pick up all the cards.

Some people try and terrorise other players by glaring into their eyes and daring them to break down uncontrollably. People with lots of bravado are good at this game, those who blush very easily may find it a little more difficult.

To play, all you need are two packs of cards.

— COLANDER GAME —

A purely verbal version of the game 'Charades'.

Each player tears a piece of paper into ten smaller pieces and writes the name of a person on each piece. They should be a mixture of fictional and real people and should be as diverse a range as possible. The papers are then folded and placed into a large bowl or colander.

To start, Player 1 takes a piece of paper from the bowl. He must try and describe the person on the paper to the person on his left. He can do anything except say the name on the paper, (impressions are allowed). Thus if the name is Bugs Bunny he might say *"ER...CARTOON RABBIT...BUCK TEETH....SAYS 'WHAT'S UP, DOC?'"*.

The best way to play is to keep on giving clues while the other player calls out responses. Players have one minute to guess as many names as they can. Once a player has guessed correctly, another paper is picked from the colander and Player 1 moves on to the next personality.
The person guessing keeps the papers and this constitutes his score.

Play proceeds round the table so, after a minute, the player who was guessing takes the colander and it is his turn to give clues to the person on his left. Play continues until there are no more papers left in the bowl.

This game can have hilarious consequences. People often think it's very funny to put in the names of obscure political leaders or foreign footballers but when they have to try and describe them to aged Aunt Nellie, it's a different matter!

If a player is really stuck with a particular name he is allowed to give up and return the paper to the pot – but valuable seconds will be lost! It is worth remembering that even if you pull out a name and have no idea as to who it is, you can always resort to 'sounds like' clues.

To play, all you need are paper, pens, a colander or a bowl and a watch with a second hand.

— DREAM TIME —

Not so much a game as a rather devious trick, Dream Time involves delving into the fantasy life of your fellow guests.

A victim is chosen and asked to leave the room. Before he leaves, tell him that while he is outside, the rest of you

will try and decide on a dream that you think he might have had. When he re-enters the room he has to try and discover the details of that dream. He can do this by asking questions, which can only be answered by *'YES'* or *'NO'*.

Once the unwitting victim has left the room, all you have to do is decide how you are going to answer the questions. For example, if the first word of the question starts with a letter between A and M in the alphabet then the answer is *"NO"*, if it starts with a letter between N and Z then the answer is *"YES"*. So you might have:

> *"WAS THERE AN ANIMAL IN THE DREAM?"* *"YES"*

> *"DID I HAVE ANY CLOTHES ON?"* *"NO"*

Alternatives could be if he looks up or down when he asks the question or whether or not he pauses in the middle of the question. Just make sure everyone is clear as to what the guidelines are. You should allow some leeway and reserve the right to answer *"MAYBE"* to a question or *"MM, THAT'S A DIFFICULT ONE, SORT OF, YES!"*. Players need to work together on this and obviously, a fair amount of bare-faced bravado is needed.

It is a cruel trick of course and players can reveal a lot about themselves this way. But if conducted in a spirit of fairness and fun I think it is forgivable.

— Guess Who? —

*A game of analogies that can raise temperatures –
see the warning below!*

One player selects another party guest, someone who is in the room, but does not tell anyone else who he has chosen. The other players have to guess who it is by asking for analogies.

> *"If he was a dog, what sort of dog would he be?"*
>
> *"What flower would he be?".*
>
> *"What sort of smell would he be?"*

Players ask questions in turn. If a player thinks he has worked out who it is then he can have a guess during his next go. If he is wrong however, he is out for the rest of that round. Whoever guesses correctly can choose the identity of the next person.

The more imaginative the categories, the better: buildings, countries, weather, sound-tracks, cars, cheeses, garden implements….nothing is out of bounds! In fact, I have known games where everyone had either guessed the identity of the person or had given up trying but was having so much fun thinking up obscure categories that the game kept going!

PUBLIC HEALTH WARNING:

This game has been known to cause nasty temper tantrums between the closest of friends. Sensitive people sometimes take offence at being likened to an over-ripe plum or a garden fork. If you wish to avoid this, or it is quite a small dinner party, you could try selecting famous personalities instead (e.g. movie stars). This should keep the peace and you can still enjoy thinking up suitable analogies but it is not as revealing, nor is it as much fun!

— HOT GOSSIP —

*A game of gossip, best played amongst players
who know each other fairly well.*

Player 1 volunteers to leave the room while everyone else
writes down a remark about him, it can be complimentary or
completely scandalous! He is then called back in and one
person reads out the remarks, one at a time. Player 1 has to
try and identify who said each remark. The first phrase might
be *"SOMEONE SAYS YOU ARE A FLIRT"*. If Player 1 can correctly
identify who that *"SOMEONE"* is, then it is that person's turn to
leave the room and become the next *"VICTIM"*.
If Player 1 guesses incorrectly then the next remark,
"SOMEONE CALLED YOU BOSSY", is read out. His ordeal continues
until he can identify the source of a particular comment.

To play, all you need are paper and pens.

— Names Of —

Quick thinking, general knowledge and a half-decent sense of rhythm are pre-requisites for this group game.

Players need to sit in a circle and a rhythm needs to be established. First of all players slap their hands on their thighs, then they clap their hands together, then they click their right fingers and finally their left. So it should go *"SLAP, CLAP, CLICK, CLICK"*.

You might need to practice this so that everyone is doing it at the same pace.

The idea is that the first person thinks of a category and then each player in turn has to give a different example, taking care only to speak in time with the clicks.

So it might go something like this:

PLAYER 1 ~	SLAP,	CLAP,	*"NAMES"*	*"OF"*
	SLAP,	CLAP,	*"CAPITAL"*	*"CITIES"*
PLAYER 2 ~	SLAP,	CLAP,	*"PA - RIS"*	
PLAYER 3 ~	SLAP,	CLAP,	*"ROME"*	
PLAYER 4 ~	SLAP,	CLAP,	*"NEW"*	*"YORK"*

and so on.

Sounds simple? Try it! There is something about the insistent rhythm that sends people's brains into a complete spin. If anyone stumbles, breaks the rhythm or is struck dumb they either lose a life or drop out of the game. The more imaginative the categories, the better the game: try 'CURRY DISHES' or 'BATHROOM OBJECTS'. The pace can be altered as and when players think fit.

— Odds On Favourite —

A fabulous and addictive bluffing game!

Every player is dealt a single card face down. On a given signal everyone picks up their card and, without looking at it, places it on their forehead. Now the fun begins.

Players take turns to bet on whether their card is the highest one. Aces are high. You can bet with matchsticks, after-dinner mints or hard currency. Obviously bluffing is the name of the game here. Snort derisively at other players' foreheads, roll your eyes in disbelief and lay your bet confidently. Eventually you will bully some poor soul into dropping out of the game and they will discover that they were holding an ace!

Be warned. This is a simple enough game to describe but, like all the best games, its tactics are many and it can be completely addictive!

To play, all you need is a pack of cards.

— QUICK ON THE DRAW —

*A hugely fashionable parlour game, much
popularised in recent years.*

Players form two teams. Each team needs to think of 12
things which it will ask the opposing team to draw and
these should be written on separate pieces of paper.
They can be objects (large or small) or mottos and sayings.
Some suggestions are given opposite, alternatively the host
could have compiled a list prior to the dinner party.

The first player in Team A is given the first object to draw. His
fellow team members have to guess what is being drawn and
should call out suggestions but, other than *"YES"* or *"NO"*, the
artist must not utter a sound. A one minute time limit is imposed
and the artist may draw as many pictures as he wishes in order
to convey the word. If the team guesses what has been drawn
within the time limit, it gains one point. Now it is Team B's turn.

This is one of those games where the meekest of people
can get quite frantic and start stabbing their pencil in the
air screaming *"IT'S OBVIOUS FOR GOD'S SAKE!!"*. You have
been warned.

To play, all you need are paper and pens.

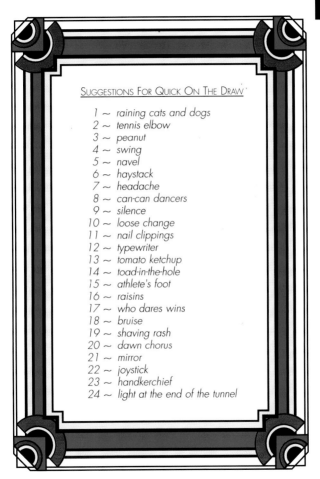

SUGGESTIONS FOR QUICK ON THE DRAW

1 ~ *raining cats and dogs*
2 ~ *tennis elbow*
3 ~ *peanut*
4 ~ *swing*
5 ~ *navel*
6 ~ *haystack*
7 ~ *headache*
8 ~ *can-can dancers*
9 ~ *silence*
10 ~ *loose change*
11 ~ *nail clippings*
12 ~ *typewriter*
13 ~ *tomato ketchup*
14 ~ *toad-in-the-hole*
15 ~ *athlete's foot*
16 ~ *raisins*
17 ~ *who dares wins*
18 ~ *bruise*
19 ~ *shaving rash*
20 ~ *dawn chorus*
21 ~ *mirror*
22 ~ *joystick*
23 ~ *handkerchief*
24 ~ *light at the end of the tunnel*

—Tricks —

*This is not so much a game, but rather a brain
teaser with which to intrigue your guests.*

A knife and fork are passed from person to person, sitting round in a circle. As you pass the cutlery on, you should say either *"THIS KNIFE AND FORK ARE CROSSED"* or *"THIS KNIFE AND FORK ARE NOT CROSSED"*. What will bewilder your guests is that what you say does not seem to depend on whether the knife and fork are actually crossed! Encourage them to join in and pass the implements round. Sometimes they will get it right and sometimes not, but they will not know why. The trick is that what you say depends on whether or not your own legs are crossed. Thus, someone with their legs crossed should say *"THIS KNIFE AND FORK ARE CROSSED"*, whether or not the cutlery is.

Gradually, people will realise the trick, leaving some poor unfortunates none the wiser and increasingly frustrated and intrigued!

A different version of this is to pass round a cigarette packet, saying *"THIS CIGARETTE PACKET IS OPEN"* or *"THIS CIGARETTE PACKET IS CLOSED."* Again, sometimes the packet is open, sometimes closed but this seems to bear no relation to what you say. It actually depends on whether the person closes his mouth after he speaks or whether it remains open! You can make up your own version of this quite easily.

To play, all you need are a knife and fork.

— Up Jenkins —

A modicum of co-ordination and a minuscule amount of brain-power are all that are needed to play this game, which is Victorian in origin hence its rather dignified name.

Players form two teams and sit opposite each other at a table.

Team A takes a coin and, with all team members' hands under the table, passes it from one to the other so that the other team has no idea where it finally rests. On a given signal, all the players in Team A bang their hands on the table, keeping their palms down. The noise will cover the sound of the coin.

Team B has to guess where the coin is. The players do this by pointing at a hand and telling its owner to *"Up, Jenkins!"*. Each time a player reveals an empty palm, Team B is awarded one point, for the object is to leave the palm containing the coin until the very last. If it succeeds, Team B hides the coin next. If the coin is revealed before all the hands have been turned over, then Team A is awarded a point and gets the chance to hide the coin again. Needless to say, poker faces are a must for this game! *To play, all you need is a coin.*

—  WINK MURDER —

Yes, it's a kids' game, but it's great fun, generating not only a great deal of suspense but also the odd nervous giggle.

You need a playing card for each player and one of the cards should be the Jack of Spades. Players draw a card each and make sure that no-one else sees it. Whoever has drawn the Jack is the murderer. The murderer kills his victims by making eye contact and winking subtly.
If a player is winked at, he should wait a few moments and then 'die' as dramatically as possible. Gradually more and more players will die off leaving the survivors increasingly tense and watchful. The others need to try and catch the murderer in the act.

The temptation here might be to stare at the floor and avoid making eye contact with anyone. However you cannot catch the murderer with this tactic as you need to intercept a wink. People who can keep a straight face and who are good at darting sidelong glances are best at this game.

A killer who is a little the worse for wear can be very amusing – discreet winks seem to become particularly difficult late at night.

To play, all you need is a pack of cards.

— ATZEE —

A very good dice game, possibly the world's greatest.

You will need five dice and should copy out the yatzee scorecard on a piece of paper. (Alternatively, feel free to photocopy page 45).

The first player rolls all five dice. He then chooses whether to score against a certain category on the card or to try and roll any number of the dice a second time. He can then roll some, or all, of the dice for a third and final time.
Once a player has rolled three times it is the end of his turn. Players must enter something in a category (though not necessarily the one they had hoped to score in) at the end of every turn.

Players can only score once in each category and play continues until all categories have been filled. If a player fails to roll dice to suit any category in which they have yet to score, he must enter nil in a category of his choice.

If scoring in the Top Section, players score the value of the dice shown. So if a player throws four fives, he can choose to enter 20 in the Fives category.

If scoring in the Lower Section, you score as indicated on the card. A throw of four fives could for instance be entered in the 4 of a Kind section - since all dice are counted in this section, the score will be higher than if the player chooses to enter a score of 20 in the Fives category.

A score of 50 can be entered in the Yatzee section for 5 of a kind (any number). A Yatzee bonus of 100 is scored if a second Yatzee is thrown. Full House is five of a kind or three' of one kind and two of another (any number/s). A Low Straight is a run of 1-2-3-4-5. A High Straight is a run of 2-3-4-5-6. The Chance section can be used at any time (though only once). A bonus of 35 is automatically scored if the total of the Top Section equals or exceeds 63.

The winner is the player with the highest score.

To play, all you need are five dice and copies of the scorecard for every player.

YATZEE SCORE CARD

TOP SECTION

Add only Ones			
Add only Twos			
Add only Threes			
Add only Fours			
Add only Fives			
Add only Sixes			
Total			
63 or more = 35 bonus			
Total of top section			

LOWER SECTION

3 of a Kind - Total All Dice			
4 of a Kind - Total All Dice			
Full House 25			
Low Straight (1-5) 30			
High Straight (2-6) 40			
YATZEE 50			
Chance Total All Dice			
2nd YATZEE 100			
Total of Lower Section			
Total of Top Section			
GRAND TOTAL			

RIOTOUS GAMES

— Adverb Game —

*A reasonably daft game that can yield
extremely amusing results.*

The host needs to have prepared a list of adverbs in advance. There are some suggestions included in case you are looking for inspiration. Each word is written on a separate piece of paper which is folded and placed in a bowl. Each player selects a word and then has to act in the manner of that word. There are two different ways in which this can be played.

One version is that one player only selects a word. He then has to do whatever the other players instruct him to do but always 'IN THE MANNER OF HIS CHOSEN WORD'. Thus a player may be asked to:

> *"WALK ROUND THE ROOM"*
>
> *"HAVE A DRINK"*
>
> *"TAKE HIS SHOES OFF"*
>
> *"ASK ANOTHER GUEST FOR A DATE"*
>
> *"SING A SONG"*

He might have to do these things 'SEXILY', 'AGGRESSIVELY' or 'CAREFULLY'. The others attempt to guess the word. Once someone does this correctly, the next player has a go.

"....*languidly*"

The best games are when someone has a ludicrously inappropriate word: watching a six foot giant attempting to tie his shoes 'DAINTILY' for example is a scream.

The other variation is that everyone chooses a word at the same time and for the next half an hour everyone has to act 'IN THE MANNER' of the word they chose. This is certainly more chaotic but individuals feel less exposed. You can also get some very interesting interactions as Mr Placid starts to infuriate Mrs Impatient and Mrs Loud terrorises Mr Shy. Players can write down what adverb they think other players have selected and compare notes at the end.

To play, all you need are paper, pens and a bowl.

SOME SUGGESTIONS FOR
THE ADVERB GAME:

SHYLY	ENERGETICALLY
LUSTILY	MANIACALLY
COYLY	OBSESSIVELY
PRUDISHLY	DISTRACTEDLY
CLUMSILY	HYSTERICALLY
LOUDLY	ENIGMATICALLY
CALMLY	HUNGRILY
FEARFULLY	DISGUSTEDLY
VAGUELY	CONDESCENDINGLY
SLYLY	BRAVELY

— CHARADES —

A timeless classic which never fails to amuse.

The Victorian version called for lots of dressing up and teams usually acted out single words broken into their component parts ("BANDAGE" or "NIGHTINGALE" for instance).
Our modern variety is a more impromptu version often played at breakneck speed!

Players form two teams. Team A gives one member of Team B the title of a book, film, play or musical. That player then has to return to his team-mates and act out the title, non-verbally until they guess it correctly. Team B can shout out suggestions and ask questions but the player 'ACTING' can only nod or shake his head - absolutely no sound is allowed!

Certain gestures are recognised. Opening and closing your palms signifies a book, circling one hand at the side of your

head signifies a film, and drawing a stage with curtains up with your hands means it's a play. Mime a singer to indicate a musical.

Players usually hold up a number of fingers to show how many words are in the title and then which word they are attempting to act out.

So it might sound like this:

"IT'S A FILM.......FOUR WORDS......THIS IS THE FOURTH WORD....".

Teams usually end up shouting out suggestions more or less continuously and things can get quite noisy. You need to impose a time limit and teams take turns at guessing.

An alternative way to play is to have an MC who thinks up titles and both teams try and guess the same title simultaneously. There is less potential embarrassment in this version as a player from each team acts out the charade at the same time but it can become chaotic and the MC needs to be on the look-out for any members eavesdropping on the opposing team!

The joy of the game lies in thinking up really challenging titles but it can be hard to know which ones are going to be difficult. How about Romans In Britain, ..Death In Venice,.. Under Milkwood, ..A Bridge Too Far, ..Quo Vadis,...Grease,.. Independence Day,...The Unbearable Lightness of Being?

To play, all you need is a watch with a second hand.

— Clumps —

*A great guessing game in which players
constantly switch teams!*

Players form two groups and take up positions in opposite
corners of a room. One person from each group goes
outside the room and together they decide upon an object.
They then re-enter the room, but each returns to the side from
which the other player came: thus, A goes to B's side and
B to A's.

Each group then fires questions at the player to try and find
out what the object is but the player can only answer "YES"
or "NO". Questions should be asked quietly so as not to
give away clues to the other side. When a team guesses
correctly, the players clap their hands and claim both players
who went out.

The game continues until one side has taken all the players
from the other and one solitary soul is left in a corner!

What you will get is lots and lots of urgent whispering followed
by a triumphant round of applause. This game certainly gets the
competitive spirit going but people may well find that they cross
from team to team! You can make it easier by deciding on a
theme (kitchen implements, mountaineering) or by restricting it to
personalities (dead or alive).

— THE DATING GAME —

*This game needs two extrovert players to do a bit of acting.
It will prove hilarious to those watching!*

The two selected sit next to each other facing the others and are given a playing card each. The value of their cards represents the strength of their desire for each other. Aces are low. The players now have to act out that desire non verbally! The task of the observers is to guess the value of the two cards dealt. If the two players are particularly confident actors you could try creating a situation for them (on a bus, in a queue for a cash machine, in the supermarket) but no words should pass their lips.

Be prepared for some startling revelations! It is amazing to see just how differently people can interpret the same card and the look of terror on a player's face when another player lurches towards them can be a joy to behold!

To play, all you need is a pack of cards.

— I SPY —

It sounds crazy, but it's fun!

Suspend either an old sheet or a roll of paper across an open doorway. You need to leave a gap at the bottom, which should be large enough to reveal either ankles and feet or, from the knee downwards: it depends on which version you decide to play!

Players form two teams; one goes outside the room, the other remains inside.

Those outside the room take off their shoes, socks and roll up their trousers if necessary. One by one, they walk up to the sheet and present their legs to the audience inside the room. The others confer and write down who they think the legs belong to! Identities are revealed at the end and the team is awarded one point for each correct guess.

I have also played a version where only the tiniest gap was left and we had to guess the identity from the sight of the toes only!

The room must be well lit otherwise people's shadows might give the game away.

If the company is mixed, it is a good idea to divide the teams

according to gender. The more people who join in, the merrier the game.

To play, all you need are paper, pens, an old sheet or a roll of paper.

— FOLLOW THE LEADER —

An action game to test a player's vigilance.

One person is sent out of the room. The others then select someone to be the leader. The leader starts performing some relatively surreptitious and repetitive task: scratching their nose, licking their teeth, tapping their foot, rolling their eyes....... etc. Everybody else follows suit. At this point the other player is called back into the room.

Players continue doing whatever it is they were doing until the leader suddenly switches to a different action. Everybody else immediately follows suit. The eagle–eyed observer has to decide who he thinks the leader is. It is not unknown for the observer to become quite frantic as the actions change in quick succession but he is unable to spot the instigator. A really clever and subtle leader can make the actions gradually more extreme but still remain anonymous. The others must be careful not to give the game away. Straight faces and a display of nonchalance are a must.

– Pass It On –

*This game is a bit like a mimed version of "Chinese Whispers";
you'll be amazed to see how the original mime changes!*

Players form two teams and one (Team B) leaves the
room. Team A then thinks of an action or sequence of
actions. It can be as mundane or dramatic as you wish,
anything from making scrambled eggs to going to the circus
and falling into a cage of lions.

A member of Team B is called into the room and one person
in Team A acts out the chosen situation. No words should be
spoken. The next member of Team B is called in and the
situation is acted out to him by his fellow team member. Play
continues until all the players are in the room and it is the task
of the unlucky last player to say what they think the situation is.

— RHYME TIME —

This game was originally known by the rather impressive name of "Dumb Crambo". It calls for some elementary mime skills and a lot of gusto!

Players form two teams; one remains inside the room, the other goes outside. Those inside the room decide upon a word, let us say they chose the word "KITE". When the others return, they give them a word which RHYMES with the chosen one: in this case, they might say "It rhymes with the word 'white'".

The other team has to guess the chosen word by acting out the various possibilities. Thus it might act out "FIGHT", "BITE", "LIGHT" etc. Players should act as a team so no one person is singled out and they are not allowed to use any words – dumb play only!

The other team can behave quite badly and reward the dramatic efforts with boos or hisses. When the team mimes the correct word it should be cheered very loudly!

LATE
NIGHT
GAMES

— ARE YOU THERE — MORIARTY?

A ridiculous game requiring little more than the ability to hit somebody with a rolled up newspaper!

Two people are blindfolded and asked to lie on their backs on the floor. They should have their toes pointing to opposite corners of the room and their heads should be about three feet apart. Each is then given a rolled up newspaper to use as a weapon.

The first player asks "ARE YOU THERE, MORIARTY?" to which the other player must answer "YES". Both players can then strike at where they think the other player's head is. Obviously the idea is to speak and then move your head as quickly as possible. Players can dodge and wriggle as much as they like but should not get up off the floor.

This is one of those games of almost sublime simplicity which is probably more fun to watch than perform! It may appear ridiculously simple on the page but has to be played to be properly appreciated.

To play, all you need are a newspaper and two blindfolds.

— ᗷALLOON ᗷASHING —

Another game of almost sublime simplicity which you shouldn't discount before having at least one go.

Each player blows up a balloon and attaches it to his ankle with a piece of string. The player can either tie it close to his ankle or leave a length of string – both options have advantages and disadvantages! Armed with some rolled up newspaper, players then have to try and burst each other's balloons whilst at the same time trying to protect their own balloons by dodging blows. Once a player's balloon is burst he should retire from the fray and watch the mayhem from the sidelines. You will probably be left with two players dancing round each other, locked in combat, laughing helplessly.

You will need a good clear starting signal as pandemonium tends to break out when this game is played. It is also a good idea to clear the room of all breakable objects in advance. It is important to stress that players cannot use their hands or any sharp instruments to burst the balloons, their only weapon is their newspaper truncheon.

This game can be extraordinarily therapeutic and exhilarating, particularly for tired-out, high-flying executives.

To play, all you need are balloons, newspapers and string.

— Contortion —

*This is best played towards the end of the evening
when all caution has been thrown to the wind.
Unless of course your friends are all extreme extroverts,
in which case it might be a suitable warm-up game!*

Each player writes the numbers one to six on separate
pieces of paper. These papers are then scattered over the
floor. The numbers must be visible.

Players then take turns to throw a dice and put their left foot on
the number that they have thrown. On the next round, players
must place their right foot on the number they throw. On the
third round, they must place their left hand on a number
(keeping their feet in place), and on the fourth round, their right
hand. If a player falls over, he is out for the rest of the game.
He can then act as an adjudicator for the rest.

If a player throws a number and all the papers with that
number on are used, he is allowed to throw again.
The adjudicator should make sure that no-one is trying to cheat
so that they end up entwined with the person of their choice!

To play, all you need are paper, pens and a dice.

— Head To Head —

A mad race which could come to a sticky end.

You will need two teams, preferably with an even number of players in each, and a start and finish line on the floor.

The first two players in each team stand at the start line facing each other with an orange held in place between their foreheads. They then have to move sideways making their way to the finish line and back again without dropping the orange. Confident players may attempt a mad dash, others may adopt a more tortuous crab-like pace. If the orange falls, not only do the players risk getting bruised foreheads, they also have to start again.

Head to Head is best played as a relay race, once back at the start line the next two players take over, but they must have the orange firmly in place before they start again.

To play, all you need are two oranges, or any other spherical objects, so long as they are not too hard.

— Nose Ball —

At last, a game for people with large noses!

You will need to mark a start and finish line on the floor. Depending on the number of players you can either get everyone to compete against each other, in which case you will need one table tennis ball per player, or you could form two teams and have a relay race, in which case you need only two table tennis balls.

Players line up on their hands and knees at the start line with their balls placed in front of them. On the word 'Go!', players push their balls forward using only their noses. You will definitely need a referee to keep a close eye on proceedings. If any player touches the ball with anything other than his nose, he has to return to the start line and begin again.

This is quite tough on the knees so be warned. However there's nothing quite as funny as watching people in their smart party clothes crawling around on their hands and knees in hot pursuit of a ping pong ball!

To play, all you need are table tennis balls.

— OBSTACLE RACE —

*This is a hilarious trick which depends on
someone being an unwitting "victim".*

If there is more than one victim, they are sent out of the room and called in, one by one. Meanwhile, the other players set up an obstacle race by placing chairs, stools and ornaments on the floor. The victim is then given a moment to study the arrangement before being blindfolded.

He has to make his way along the course without being able to see. What he does not know, however, is that while he was being blindfolded, the other players quietly removed all the obstacles!

It is very funny to watch the player carefully picking his way round the non-existent objects and even funnier, to see his face when the blindfold is removed!

To play, all you need are a blindfold and plenty furniture props.

— Orange Game —

Originally a children's game, this will nonetheless provide much hilarity for adults!

Players form two teams and stand in a line. On a given signal players start to pass an orange down the line. However, they must do so by holding the orange under their chins – no hands are allowed. The transfer of the orange from one chin to another is obviously critical; the angle must be right and this is not helped if people are laughing convulsively! If the orange is dropped, it is returned to the start of the line.

Variations include passing the orange from feet to feet. In this version, players sit in chairs with their legs held out straight in front of them. Players hold the orange between their ankles and need to perfect a sort of 'SEMI TOSS' in order to pass it effectively. This version entails less bodily contact and is slightly more sedate.

To play, all you need are two oranges.

— Sardines —

An adult version of hide and seek!

Obviously you will need a certain amount of space in which to play this, a one bedroom flat does not offer

many hiding places but it is surprising just how imaginative people can be!

One person goes off to hide while the rest of the assembled company continue their convivial conversation. After five minutes the next person gets up to look for the hideaway but must do this alone. When he finds the person (hidden under a bed, in a wardrobe or whatever) he then has to squeeze himself into the same hiding place. Thus the game continues. As you can imagine in no time at all you have most of the party crammed into a corner, jostling elbows and trying to stifle give-away giggles while some lone soul looks for them.

If your house is exceptionally large you could try sending everyone off at once to find the hidden person. If a player finds him, he has to try and join him without giving the game away to the other players. This does add a certain frisson to the game but is virtually impossible if everyone is searching in the same room!

A WORD OF CAUTION HERE: there is an apocryphal story about an unpopular guest who was sent off to hide and nobody bothered to try and find him. The poor unfortunate man spent the whole evening lurking behind the fridge freezer. This is not a practice to be proud of. However it does mean that you should not be surprised if your guests appear somewhat reluctant to be the first to start this game off.

— STRING ALONG —

This is a great game to play at the end of the evening –
it helps if players are wearing casual clothes.

Players form two teams and stand in a line. The player at the head of each team holds a ball of string, attached to the end of which, is a spoon.

On the word "Go", the first player passes the spoon down his shirt, through his trousers or shorts and on to the next player. Play passes rapidly from player to player, all the time more string is being released from the ball.

When the spoon reaches the end of the line, play is reversed. Players pass the spoon back up their trousers and shirt and hand it back.

The first team to finish with its ball of string re-wound is the winner.

To play, all you need are string and two spoons.

— SQUEAK PIGGY SQUEAK —

*If you think this game sounds ridiculous, well you're right, it is.
But it's amazing just how much fun a group
of adults can have playing it - particularly if alcohol has been
consumed and/or there are any unspoken passions
smouldering amongst your guests!*

The more players the better, you certainly need a minimum of six.

Everyone takes a chair and sits in a circle. Everyone, that is, except one person who is blindfolded and made to stand in the middle. Make sure the blindfold is not see-through – it sounds obvious but it has been known! The person should be given a cushion and then, in the time honoured fashion of all the best blindfold games, turned round a few times until he is thoroughly disorientated.

The "PIGGY IN THE MIDDLE" then has to make his way towards one of the guests. Once he has chosen someone, he has to carefully place the cushion on their lap and clamber on top. When he is sitting comfortably on top of the cushion, he issues the command: "SQUEAK PIGGY SQUEAK".

The chosen guest then has to squeak three times, preferably without collapsing into giggles. If the blindfolded player can correctly identify the person making the squeaks then the two players swap positions.

It is a good idea for players seated in the circle to change places between every round.

Some people take this game very seriously and go to quite extraordinary lengths to disguise their squeaks. Of course, if you have a very large person sitting on your lap then your voice will automatically sound somewhat different. It is important to point out that the voice should be the only clue given – no groping for clues allowed! *To play, all you need are a blindfold and cushion.*

OTHER TITLES AVAILABLE FROM LAGOON BOOKS:

GIFT BOOKS
OPTICAL ILLUSIONS AND PUZZLES	(ISBN 1899712402)
MIND-BOGGLERS- bizarre but amazingly true trivia!	(ISBN 1899712445)
X IS FOR UNEXPLAINED	(ISBN 1899712259)

QUIZ BOOKS
WHERE IN THE WORLD AM I? - Mystery Geography Quiz	(ISBN 1899712410)
PUB TRIVIA QUIZ	(ISBN 189971250X)
SPORTS TRIVIA QUIZ	(ISBN 1899712267)
WHO IN THE WORLD AM I? - Mystery Celebrity Quiz	(ISBN 1899712275)

All books can be ordered from bookshops by quoting the above ISBN numbers.
Some titles may not be available in all countries. All titles are available in the UK.

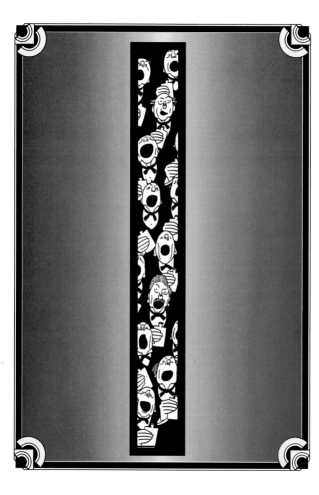